MW00633666

The Heart

of a

First Lady

A Practical Guide for the Pastor's Wife
Revised Edition

Yolanda G. Butler

First Lady Butler Ministries

Fort Worth, Texas

© Copyright 2013 by Yolanda G. Butler
© Copyright Revised Edition 2017 by Yolanda G. Butler

The Heart of a First Lady
By Yolanda G. Butler

Printed in the United States of America

ISBN-10: 1948339331
ISBN-13: 9781948339339

Published by First Lady Butler Ministries
Fort Worth, Texas 76115

All rights reserved solely by the author. The author guarantees all contents are original and do not infringe upon the legal rights of any other person or work. No part of this book may be reproduced, stored in a retrieval system, or transmitted in any form or by any means, electronic, mechanical, digital, photocopy, recording, or any other, except the brief quotations in printed reviews, without the prior written permission from First Lady Butler Ministries, POB 60087, Fort Worth, Texas 76115. For information about activities of First Lady Butler Ministries, visit our website at www.firstladybutlerministries.com.

All Scripture quotations, unless otherwise indicated, are from the HOLY BIBLE, Kings James Version (KJV). Public domain.

Scripture quotations are taken from The Living Bible copyright © 1971. Used by permission of Tyndale House Publishers, Inc., Carol Stream, Illinois 60188. All rights reserved.

Scripture quotations marked (NLT) are taken from the Holy Bible, New Living Translation, copyright © 1996, 2004, 2007 by Tyndale House Foundation. Used by permission of Tyndale House Publishers, Inc., Carol Stream, Illinois 60188. All rights reserved.

Scripture taken from The Message. Copyright © 1993, 1994, 1995, 1996, 2000, 2001, 2002. Used by permission of NavPress Publishing Group.

Cover Image credit: <a href='http://www.123rf.com/photo_8345094_a-purple-hearts-valentines-day-background-with-silver-hearts-and-flowers-on-a-darker-graduated-backg.html'>mhprice / 123RF Stock Photo</a>

Dedication

Dedicated to the memory of my dear sweet grandmother,
Sallie Pipkins McMillon,
who lived to be 104 years old and served not only as a
Pastor's Wife but as the greatest example of a true
Proverbs 31 woman in my life.

In Grateful Acknowledgement

I extend love and appreciation to my amazing husband, Bishop Donald H. Butler, who lovingly gives me the freedom to be me in every way possible.

To my children, grandchildren, and entire family, for always supporting me.

To Dr. Naddie Conedy, for sharing priceless words of wisdom with me as a young Pastor's Wife.

To the late First Lady Charlene Jamison, who gave me my very first gift as a Pastor's Wife that I cherish and share with other Pastors' Wives to this day.

To First Lady, Mother JoAnn Washington, for your example of true resilience, the strength of character, and beauty.

To First Lady, Mother Bobbie Castleberry, for being a God-given Spiritual Mother in my life.

Table of Contents

Forward
By
Mother JoAnn Washington

A must-read for every First Lady just beginning or seasoned. This book is informative, instructional and easy to read. It gives the First Lady a manual that lets her know her journey is not one that is unrecognized. This book speaks from the heart of a First Lady to other First Ladies. There is nothing like the voice of experience. I invite every Pastor's Wife to take the time to read this book. It will be one that you will need in your ministry. You have been predestined to this position of honor as a First Lady. This book will give you a clue of what it all entails.

Mother Washington is the First Lady of Rose of Sharon Ministries, Fort Worth, Texas, and has served as a First Lady for over 30 years with her husband.

Forward
By
Mother Bobbie Castleberry

First Lady Yolanda Butler has picked the right time in our history to write a book on *"The Heart of the First Lady."* This book delighted me, and I received encouragement knowing that the struggle is normal. Lady Butler is a seasoned Pastor's Wife who has done ministry in just about every setting possible. She offers practical advice based on her personal and spiritual walk with God. She knows how to live and walk gracefully in the spotlight as well as in the background of her husband. This book is a labor of love from one Pastor's Wife to another.

Mother Castleberry is the First Lady of Golden Gate COGIC, Fort Worth, Texas, and has served as a First Lady for over 28 years.

Introduction

The life of a Pastor's Wife (also affectionately known as the First Lady) is a calling placed upon a woman who possesses qualities within her to not only assist her husband, the Pastor but also serve the flock God has entrusted into the hands of the man of God. My years of experience in ministry as a Pastor's Wife have afforded me the opportunity to see the unique qualities that God places in the heart of the First Lady.

When my husband and I married, we were both young. He was already a minister and he fully informed me while we were courting that one day he knew he would be a pastor. Neither of us had any idea that would be just two months after marriage. Not only was I faced with having to learn what it means to be a wife but now I also had to learn what it means to be the First Lady. I had no guide, no mentor, and no spiritual mother and there were little to no resources out there. I was clueless. I jumped in the water without a life jacket or life support system. The very thing I desired--a mentor--the Lord prepared me to become, a Pastor's Wife Mentor.

This book is written to help you my sister recognize that you are not by yourself and to provide you with a few essential tools to help you in your journey as the gifted and anointed First Lady that God has called you to be. I have had the privilege of meeting and embracing many Pastors' Wives in my years of ministry, from the beginning to the seasoned. I have gleaned from their examples of wisdom and grace. No book can contain the solution to every situation a Pastor's Wife may encounter, as no two Pastors' Wives are alike, and every house is different and unique in and of itself.

Throughout this book, I will refer to Pastor's Wife and First Lady interchangeably but they are one and the same, although I believe the term "First Lady" has a more endearing quality to it.

May this resource be an encouragement to you to fulfill every intricate detail of your life that God has endowed you with, and may others embrace the priceless value of your heart as a First Lady.

Chapter 1

Definition of a First Lady

"Many daughters have done virtuously, but thou
excellest them all." (Prov. 31:29 KJV)

By definition in an ecclesiastical context, the First Lady is the wife of the Senior Pastor of the Church. She is also called the Pastor's Wife. No, you will not find either term in the Bible but her qualities are definitely defined. She is the wife of one husband. (I Tim. 3:2) She is to love, respect, be submissive, and be the number one supporter of her husband. (Titus 2:4-5; Eph. 5:22, Col. 3:18) She is to love, nurture and train her children. (Titus 2:4) She is to present herself before others tastefully and modestly. (I Tim. 2:9) She must endeavor to be careful and wise in her speech and action. (Titus 2:5) She is to embrace her femininity and virtuosity (Titus 2:5, Prov. 31:10) because so many women need to see an example of what it means to be "a lady" in the pure sense of what God created her (and you) to be.

She possesses the transforming and influential power as the keeper of her own home. (Titus 2:5; Prov. 31:27) She is skilled to do good. (Titus 2:5; Heb. 13:15) She is a teacher, advisor and wise counselor to the women. (Titus 2:3, Prov. 14:1). She is one given to prayer, supplication, and intercession. (Eph. 6:18)

Now please do not stress out and convince yourself that you cannot measure up to these qualities. If God has called your husband to be a Pastor, so has He called you to walk in your customized shoes as a Pastor's Wife, the First Lady. You got the goods, my sister. Some aspects are probably clear to you and some may not be, but rest assured they are intricately woven into your personality. Part of your salvation requires that you work daily to maintain it. The same applies to you as a Pastor's Wife. You never stop working and developing you into a better person for the Kingdom. You are a unique you who just happens to be a First Lady and there is no one else like you.

Chapter 2

The Pastor and the First Lady

*"Her husband can trust her and she will
greatly enrich his life." (Prov. 31:11, NLT)*

It is important to recognize and respect the fact that God called your husband into the office of the Pastor, the shepherd of God's people. He is fundamentally responsible for the growth, stagnation, and decline of the ministry. His calling is unique to no one else within the church, including you. As God's under-shepherd, he has been endowed with a vision unique to his personality, calling, talents and spiritual gifts. He has been endowed with the grace (ability to perform) to function in this capacity to take oversight of God's people with care, nurture, patience, firmness, and a loving hand. God has gifted him to know the personality and heart of every member.

God established the humanistic order when he created man first and then woman. Christ is the head of every man, man is the head of a woman, and God is the head of Christ. (I Cor. 11:3) Thus, an order is established pertaining to a pastor and his wife. Christ is the head of the pastor, and the pastor is the head of the pastor's wife. If you understand, respect and embrace this role, then you will find you can walk in greater harmony with your husband, the Pastor.

Whether you agree with it or not, your husband, the Pastor, is the final authority in all matters, spiritually and naturally, concerning the church. He often has to make decisions based on the "whole" of the matter rather than the "part" of the matter. While your inclination is to deal with it NOW, the Pastor often has to wait before addressing an issue.

Often the dynamics and the timing may not be right and could be more damaging than effective to the body of Christ. (My husband, Bishop Butler, has written a book *"Understanding Church Dynamics"* that gives greater insight into the fundamentals of church dynamics.) You may recognize an error and your husband, the Pastor, may not be willing to adhere to what you have to say. So what do you do? Pray, pray, and pray again.

The greatest discipline you are going to learn is when to be silent and when to speak. (Ecc. 3:7) Whichever season it is, you always pray. Prayer harnesses your emotions and keeps you humbled. You will find that your prayers can invoke a greater change in the heart of the man of God (your husband) and you than an unending battle of wills.

God has gifted my hand with many talents including Administration, Music, and Ministering. I am blessed in that

Bishop Butler allows me to share much weight in the ministry with him. I am the Church Administrator. While I am responsible for the Administration of the Church, Bishop Butler, the Senior Pastor, still has the final authority and say-so in all matters.

I am often consulted by our Finance Department concerning the church finances and try to keep much of this burden off my husband's shoulders. However, decisions that supersede my scope of authority or those generally not done within the course of the church functionality, I must consult the Senior Pastor for the final decision.

When I served as the Minister of Music, I was responsible for the flow and selection of all music for all programs held at the church. Notwithstanding, if there was anything that the Senior Pastor disapproved of, I had to respect his decision and ensure the Music Department conformed accordingly.

"Obey them that have the rule over you, and submit yourselves: for they watch for your souls, as they that must give account, that they may do it with joy, and not with grief: for that is unprofitable for you." (Heb. 13:17)

It is humbling to know that neither you nor I am exempt from this powerful Scripture on submission. He may be your husband but when he steps into the role of the shepherd, he is your pastor.

Chapter 3

The First Lady's Mantle

*"For it is God which worketh in you both to will
and to do of his good pleasure." (Philip. 2:13)*

The word "mantle" means covering, an important role or responsibility. True to your calling as a First Lady is that you set the tone and example for the women of your local church body, both young and old alike. Eyes are constantly fixed and focused on you. There are those who will glean from your example in character, style, and dress. It is the mantle that has been bestowed on your life and God designed you to style it well. Understand that what you say, how you say it, when you say it, and what you do not say are all examined. I guess there exists some inexplicable code that you, your children and your husband are supposed to be the personification of perfect happiness, joy, love, and peace in the Holy Ghost devoid of problems, circumstances and outward distractions.

There are high expectations placed not just on you but also on your entire family. Do not let that trip you out. If you do, it will wear you down. The people of God and especially the women will look to you for strength. Your presence, smile, and demeanor really do carry weight. This is why prayer is such an essential aspect of the life of a Pastor's Wife, discussed later in this book. You daily pour into the lives of others and it is vital to your tenacity and feminality (the quality of being feminine with personality) that you ask God to pour back into you and equip you to fulfill your role as a woman, wife, mother and Pastor's Wife, not fake, but from a genuine servant's heart. This is the First Lady's Mantle.

I know this may seem overwhelming and the question, *"What have I gotten myself into"* may cross your mind more often than enough. Let me help you. As a First Lady, God has adorned you with your own mantle that sets you apart from every other woman in the house that you and your husband are called to serve. You are the fragrance of the house. You are called to not just wear it but wear it well. Your calling is unique to no one else within the church. If God has called and anointed your husband, the Pastor, so has he called you and anointed you to be the Pastor's Wife.

As a Pastor's Wife, you have been endowed with qualities that compliment your husband's heart according to your personality, calling, talents, and spiritual gifts. Let me assure you that God has endowed you with the grace (ability to perform) to function in this capacity. This is the First Lady's Mantle. Let no one persuade you otherwise for you will be challenged. Just as the Senior Pastor is the Spiritual Father of the Church, so are you the Spiritual Mother, having the ability to be caring, nurturing, understanding, compassionate, patient and loving. This is the First Lady's Mantle. You often will see things that your husband will not see from the eyes as a Spiritual Mother. This is the First Lady's Mantle.

In all that this mantle encompasses there is one aspect you must always remember: Never, ever, ever, lose your identity in who you are as a woman. Just because you are a Pastor's Wife does not mean you lose your personality. You do not become lost in your husband or anyone else for that place belongs only to God. Galatians 2:20 states, *"I am crucified with Christ: nevertheless I live; yet not I, but Christ liveth in me: and the life which I now live in the flesh I live by the faith of the Son of God, who loved me, and gave himself for me." (KJV)*

We do not live because of our husbands. We live because of Christ who gives us the ability to live and love our husbands, our children, and our family, the household of faith, our neighbors, and even our enemies. You are to perform and function as God designed you to by the grace and favor over your life. This is the First Lady's Mantle. Yes, you will find that your greatest desire is to promote the success of your husband as a Pastor. However, I caution you to not lose you in the midst of all your pouring. If you take no time to build you and enhance you, you will find yourself becoming worn out, empty, lifeless and vulnerable to the enemy's spirit of immobilization (discussed later in this book).

Your style also includes your unique ministry. It is your personal contribution to the church ministry. Do not be afraid to work this aspect in the church. You will, of course, need the approval of your husband in order to go forward. It may even take time to develop and you will even have to "prove" yourself before your husband can be confident that you are ready to work the ministry. This is not being cruel to you but actually protecting you.

I have been saved for over 37 years but have not worked in ministry that entire time. I have been serving as a Pastor's Wife for over 33 years but I did not accept my calling as an Evangelist until nearly 13 years *after* becoming a Pastor's Wife. Why? Because I was not ready! Yes, I had talents, gifts,` and a call upon my life but remember I told you I married young, had two young children, worked full-time, and was still trying to figure out my role as a Pastor's Wife. I did not even chair the Women's Department. I had some grooming, pruning, and processing to go through including a season of depression. I would come to learn later in life just how immature I was and needed much rebuilding.

In the meantime, until God brings you to completion in the area that he has called you to, continue to wear your mantle and wear it well.

"Humble yourself therefore under the mighty hand of God, that he may exalt you in due season." (I Peter 5:5 KJV)

In doing this, God will blossom you. Your actions and the anointing God places in your life will define and solidify your call that no man can dispute.

Chapter 4

The First Family

"Train up a child in the way he should go, and when he is old, he will not depart from it." (Prov. 22:6 KJV)

As a Pastor's Wife, you may find yourself in a position more often than enough where you feel like you have to constantly fight for your family, your children, your husband and even you. I understand. It is so hurting when others talk about your children and your husband who all have sacrificed so much for the ministry and the people of the Lord. You play a very vital role here as wife and mother.

While you and your husband are called to serve in ministry, your young children have no understanding of this yet. More important to the lives of your children is Dad and Mom, not Pastor and First Lady. Proverbs 22:6 is not a guarantee prescription that your children will always serve God even if, God forbid, they happen to stray away. However, it is a charge to the parents to be parents in their children's lives by creating an atmosphere of learning, growing, and cultivating in a balanced manner, e.g., education, academic, Biblical training, moral training, etc.

It is important to try to create an atmosphere as best as you can where your children can have balance and know the difference between being a child versus a preacher's kid. Supporting them in school, extracurricular activities and other activities outside of the church walls is just as important as supporting them in Sunday School, the Easter program, and the Church Christmas play. A family vacation is just as important as the Church picnic. You teach them balance and priorities. You demonstrate that there is life outside the church. You live it and demonstrate it to them. You teach them good time management skills by being on time for school and work just like you teach them to be on time for church.

My husband and I jointly parented our children, instilling the Word in their lives, living it, and showing them the importance of choices. We then stepped back, trusted that we did the best to our ability, and watched them write their own pages of life. They made some mistakes but also made some magnificent achievements. Today our children have embraced their own as solid citizens in the world and also their personal call to ministry.

When our son became engaged, I took some time to share with his fiancée about becoming part of the "First Family." I unveiled to her what she can expect to encounter as a member of the First Family. The one thing I wanted her to remember was that at the end of the day your immediate family is your greatest ministry. Do all that you can to maintain peace and keep harmony in your home with your husband and your children. When all others are against you, you will find your greatest strength comes from the influence you have created in the sanctity of your own home. The First Family gains its strength when we remember not to neglect the importance of family first.

I had a similar conversation with our daughter's fiancée, who came from a large family that served in ministry. Because he chose to serve with us in ministry, it was important to share with him some intimate aspects of ministry and potential attacks that could rise up because he chose to marry the pastor's daughter.

Bishop and I are so proud to have an amazing daughter-in-love and son-in-love who absolutely adore our son and daughter. They have given us some rather incredible grandchildren too.

At one point, we all lived under the same roof. It brought forth some challenges. I saw how the enemy was trying to bring division amongst us. I fought and cried out to the Lord many nights in prayer for my family. I'll never forget the day we sat at the family table to discuss these challenges only to discover some emotional scars these precious young people were carrying. That family table brought forth release, forgiveness, and healing. That family table has become very important to us not just for family gatherings but for strength, laughter, and support. As a First Family, I pray that in the midst of life's challenges and busyness that you endeavor to always return back to the family table.

Chapter 5

The Enemy of the First Lady

"For we wrestle not against flesh and blood, but against principalities, against powers, against the rulers of the darkness of this world, against spiritual wickedness in high places."
(Eph. 6:12 KJV)

I have observed over time a great enemy in the life of the Pastor's Wife. It can come in any form and through any person, even the one closest to you. It is a vicious attack that is meant to stop you from functioning as a total woman in body, mind, and spirit. It is the spirit of immobilization. This is what God forewarned us when he told Eve, *"And I will put enmity between thee and the woman, and between thy seed and her seed; it shall bruise thy head, and thou shalt bruise his heel."* (Gen. 3:15 KJV).

The woman was chosen to produce life and not just in childbearing. A woman can walk into a room and change the entire atmosphere without speaking a word. (Esther 5:2) A woman's touch can comfort a child. A woman's voice can establish the tone in her home. (Prov. 21:9) Understand that your greatest enemy is not people. It is spiritual forces whose function is to prevent you from functioning in what you were created to do--be productive. It is meant to cause you to remove your mantle, set it aside, and sit in a corner lifeless and wasted. It is a spirit of depression, an oppressive and dark spirit. I have experienced it and it is nothing pleasant. It is a spirit of darkness that tries to boldly come between you and everything attached to you, be it your husband, your family or your church family. It will make its presence known often following some type of trauma in your life such as death, burn out, promiscuity, addiction, shame, guilt, rejection, abandonment, loneliness, lack of love, etc. It is a spirit of heaviness that surrounds you and blinds you from vision and reality.

Combating a spirit of immobilization mandates that as a Pastor's Wife you must guard your heart through daily meditation of the Word and prayer. Saturate yourself such that this becomes a natural part of your lifestyle. Before you start your day, make certain you cover yourself with the Word and prayer. Listen to worship music. These are anti-defense mechanisms against the attacks of the enemy.

Paul said, *"In everything give thanks for this is the will of God concerning you through Christ Jesus."* (I Thess. 5:18 KJV) This means to train your mind to develop a habit to always look to God through good times and bad times so that "life" does not wipe you out.

There is absolutely nothing odd about you being cautious as to who you allow in your inner circle. You do have to be careful who you share your thoughts with especially if it is personal and relates to your husband and your family. This is guarding your heart but leave just enough room for God to send you a trusted friend and a mentor in your life. You are not always meant to stand alone. This is why I strongly urge you to prayerfully seek God to divinely connect you with a Kingdom Sister and/or Spiritual Mother, discussed later in this book.

Chapter 6

When The First Lady Prays

"Pray without ceasing." (I Thess. 5:17 KJV)

A lifestyle of prayer and worship are essential to your survival not just as a Pastor's Wife but as a woman. You will find yourself bathing just about every situation, circumstance, and dilemma in prayer. My family and I are originally from California. After 23 years of ministry, the Lord called us to relocate to Texas, a land in which we knew absolutely no one, not even an enemy. Not only did the Lord change our location but he changed every aspect of our lives in family and ministry. This drastic transition proved to be a redefining moment for me in the realm of developing an intensive intercessory prayer life. We were placed in some tight situations where we could find no solution but in the resolution of prayer.

You cannot share everything with everyone, especially amongst the parishioners. You will find that there are truly some things that you alone must take to the Lord in your secret place behind the veil. Your relationship with the Father will intensify and your faith will increase as you see God working all things out for your good according to His purpose in Christ Jesus. (Rom. 8:28)

After many years in ministry, one of the greatest gifts the Lord has ever given to me as a Pastor's Wife is a prayer partner. I suggest you prayerfully seek the Lord to connect you with a prayer partner who is also a Pastor's Wife because you both can identify with each other.

Your prayer partner is not your gossip partner, your best friend, or your shopping buddy. In fact, a prayer partner should ideally be someone you do not see every day. The whole purpose of a prayer partner is to pray and intercede for one another. There should be very little dialogue between the two of you because you want to leave freedom for the Holy Spirit to guide your time of prayer. Establish a fixed time and endeavor to be committed to it, respecting the schedule of each other.

My prayer partner and I pray in the early morning hours Monday through Friday. We alternate days and begin with a Scripture, praying for about 30 minutes. We share prayer requests to agree on but for the most part, we allow the Holy Spirit to lead us. (Rom 8:14)

From this praying relationship developed a very strong covenant sister-relationship where we keep each other covered in prayer, even beyond our prayer time. So special is our

Kingdom connection that we made a commitment to hold each other accountable to one another and remain humble before the Lord in the work He has commissioned in our lives.

Until such a time as the Lord favors you with a prayer partner, know that the Holy Spirit is always an available prayer partner. Establish your set time with Him and watch God perform the miraculous in your life because you took the time to pray.

I invite you to the First Ladies Monday Prayer Call 6AM CST hosted by Lady Phyliss Cage of Hammond Louisiana, founder of God's Leading Ladies Empowerment Ministry. For more information, please visit the GLLEM website at www.gleadingladiesministry.net.

Chapter 7

The First Lady's Ambassador

"A wicked messenger falls into trouble but a faithful ambassador brings health." (Prov. 13:17 NKJV)

Vital to your strength and sanctity of mind is connecting with a seasoned Pastor's Wife who you and your husband can trust to provide you with godly counsel, wisdom, instruction, prayer, and support. She is someone who is a woman of proven integrity, very clear that she does not have time for foolishness (because her time is just as valuable as yours), and a teacher of good things. She is your ambassador, one who is a Kingdom spokeswoman who will only speak sound counsel, spiritually and naturally, directly to you. She will only promote God's agenda. As such, you must humble yourself and be willing to let her know up front that she has free access with no holds barred to reprove you (to tell one's faults), rebuke you (to tell it to you straight) and exhort you (to comfort and instruct) with all longsuffering.

A Pastor's Wife Ambassador is one who has the ability to teach you 1) how to love, respect, and submit to your husband, 2) love, pray and rear your children, 3) use good judgment in daily affairs, 4) understand the transforming power you possess as the keeper of your own home, and 5) be temperate in your will and emotions. (See Titus 2:4-5)

It is very important to make it clear in the beginning of this Mentor-Mentee type relationship of the access you have with your Mentor and your commitment to listen, prayerfully consider the counsel, and then adhere to the wise counsel, whether it hurts your feelings or not. Your Ambassador should not have to seek after you but rather you should seek after her for she carries what you need.

Let me make this abundantly clear: Your Ambassador is not your girlfriend, your best buddy, your pal or your friend. She is your spiritual counselor chosen to develop you to discover the fullness of who you are as a woman, wife, mother and Pastor's Wife.

If you do not have an Ambassador (Mentor), then I encourage you to pray to the Lord to divinely connect you with one. I promise you, she is out there praying for daughters like you to pour into the wisdom God has entrusted to her. While I am a mentor to Pastors' Wives, I recognize that I am not called to every Pastor's Wife but hope you endeavor to connect with other Kingdom Sisters you can glean support from and vice versa. Contact my ministry office if you need guidance in locating a Mentor or Pastors' Wives' Support Ministry in your area.

Chapter 8

A First Lady's Wish List

"For we would not, brethren, have you ignorant of our trouble which came to us in Asia, that we were pressed out of measure, above strength, insomuch that we despaired even of life."
(2 Cor. 1:8 KJV)

You may recall I mentioned how I became a wife and Pastor's Wife within two months of each other. I was a naive, twenty-one year old who had no idea what was ahead of her. I have been young but now that I am older, I want to impart a few wisdom nuggets to you that I wish I had known as a young First Lady just starting. Certainly, this wish list is not exhaustive but I pray these exhortations serve as a guidepost to help you walk much easier and wiser as a First Lady.

"But you, dear friends, must build each other up in your most holy faith, pray in the power of the Holy Spirit, and await the mercy of our Lord Jesus Christ, who will bring you eternal life. In this way, you will keep yourselves safe in God's love." (Jude 20-21 NLT)

1. There are darts/attacks that are intended for your husband that you will find yourself blocking and taking for him. Remember God will never place more on you than what He knows you can handle. (1 Cor. 10:13)

2. The parishioners may forget that you are the First Lady and be disrespectful to you. It may hurt for a moment but do not dwell on it. Put on the garment of forgiveness. Love and pray for those that stride against you. (Mat. 5:44-45)

3. There may be moments in which your husband takes his frustration out on you, even publicly. (By frustration I am not talking about abuse.) It is not personal, really it is not. It just means that he is weighty right now and because you are the closest one to him, you become the dump bag. When this happens, tell yourself, "Code Quiet!" Quietly take all that he dumped on you to your secret closet, lay it before the Lord, bathe it in prayer, leave it there, and trust God to lighten your husband's load. (Matt. 6:6)

4. Those that serve with you in one season may not serve with you in the next season. Why? Because the church has a revolving door. Relationships are seasonal, some short-term and some long-term. People leave for various reasons: misunderstanding, hurt, disappointment, anger, no reason, before their time, etc. Regardless of the reason, strengthen yourself and your husband for the ministry shall recover and go on. (Neh. 6:9)

5. Your husband, the Pastor, is going to have to deal with some issues pertaining to female parishioners that may make you feel uncomfortable. In a day in time in which pastors, the board of directors and churches are being sued for sexual misconduct, I would hope that your husband would include you in on any session where he has to speak with a female parishioner. This certainly is practiced by my husband and me. However, if you sense something "not right," know how to humbly approach your husband about using wisdom. (Prov. 15:1)

6. There will be times in which you and your family will go without for the sake of sustaining the ministry. These are called the "lean times" of ministry. As a woman, you have the gift to adapt and make the best of any situation. The greatest compliment my daughter testified of her parents is that *"If we had financial struggles, I never knew it. We were always fed, spent family time together, and neatly groomed. I always looked forward to shopping at Payless for shoes!"* Consider the sacrifice made by the family for the ministry a seed sown because God promises in his Word that He shall give a greater return. (Luke 6:38) His Word cannot lie. You shall reap your due right harvest.

7. There will be moments in which you feel you have no support from anyone, not even your husband. Abandon yourself in prayer (the place where you can pour out your heart to God), worship (the place where God's glory and your strength reside) and praise (the place where victory resides). (Ps. 42)

8. There is a price to the call for the First Family. Not everyone understands this and that is okay. What matters is that you understand the call and the cost. Let nothing separate you from the will of the Lord for God promised that He has a way of causing all things to come together and work out for your good according to His will through Christ Jesus. (Rom 8:28).

Chapter 9

When a First Lady Hurts

"Great peace have they which love thy law:
And nothing shall offend them." (Psalm 119:165)

Unresolved hurt can paralyze you as a woman. As a Pastor's Wife, we are often privy to some intimate secrets within the ministry even without our husbands sharing them with us. I believe the Holy Spirit endows us to see things that often go unnoticed by even our husbands. It is not to make us any better than he. Rather, it is to propel us into a place of intimacy with the Father in prayer. However, it is these things that we have seen and witnessed that often have a way of cutting through the very fiber of who we are as a woman.

Hurt can happen anywhere, yet it seems to magnify to a greater extent in the body of Christ. I often wondered why hurt that occurs in the church seems to have such a greater blow than others. It is because of the spiritual connection that we have as sisters and brothers in Christ that no other creature on earth has that makes *"church hurt"* so deep.

You will experience hurt more often than you deserve. It comes out of nowhere and even from those who you allowed into your private, personal space. Your immediate response often is to shut it down and shut them out. Hurt can even foster up some deep-seated, hidden issues within your own life that you thought were healed. Because we love our husbands and children so much, we will do whatever is necessary to protect them. But what do you do when you now become the victim of hurt, not once, but time after time? Do you retaliate? Do you let it slide? Do you hold it in? *"Pray about it"* just does not seem to be the cure-all when your heart is so broken.

Hurt must be dealt with. It is not meant to linger in your life for life. Lingering hurt cripples. It will become difficult for you to minister life to others when your life has been wounded so deeply just for being the Pastor's Wife. Lingering hurt develops into unresolved issues. Unresolved issues testify that there are some root aspects of your life that are vague and unsettled.

Hurt is nurtured through unfulfilled expectations, unhealed hurts, and unmet needs. An unfulfilled expectation such as the mentor relationship between the Apostle Paul and John Mark. An unhealed hurt such as the family blood relationship between Esau and Jacob that lingered for twenty-one years before reconciliation and healing took place. Then there are the unmet needs such as the business transaction between King David and business owner Nabal that had the potential to destroy two families.

How you handle an unresolved issue will 1) testify to your character (integrity), 2) expose your walk or level of maturity in God, and 3) determine the outcome of your future. God's Word tells us that our walk should reflect His standard of love, holiness, and righteousness. The Bible is very direct and as God's daughter, you have the responsibility to walk wisely and "circumspectly," and not as a "fool," making the most of every opportunity presented before you. (See Eph. 5:15-16).

The word "circumspectly" in the Greek means to walk with diligent carefulness, sensibly, and thoughtfully, not lacking wisdom. This is very powerful. It is a command that God would not have given if He did not endow us to walk in it. This means there should be a level of confidence in knowing who you are, whose you are, and where you are going. Interestingly, this word also means "perfect," meaning God expects us to attain levels of maturity each and every day. Consequently, issues or unresolved hurts that plague you are not meant to become permanent ornaments in your life.

Unresolved hurt can hover over your life so much to the point where it becomes difficult to be the unique woman that you are. Your Creator took thought when he skillfully handcrafted you to be the exceptional lady that you are. When it comes to fulfilling your various roles—wife, mother, evangelist, prophetess, entrepreneur, sister, daughter, etc.— you cannot do this in your own strength. The enemy knows this. This is why he comes after you to steal, kill and destroy every fiber of who you are, not at your high point but at your low point.

Apostle Peter said we must be on guard, and be diligent in our walk because the enemy comes with a big roar seeking the vulnerable prey to devour. (1 Peter 5:8) The adversary wants to render you lifeless. Here you are with all the goods but no spark to get going. Here it is your husband needs you, but you are hurting so badly, you can barely function. Your children want "Mommy" but your pieces are so scattered you can barely give them half of you. You know you have a calling on your life but how can you help someone else when you are bleeding so badly.

I submit to you precious one that God did not equip you to bear such a heavy burden. Men were created to work and after the fall, God added "hard" to their work ethic. There is a level of heaviness that a man must and is equipped to handle. Your level of heaviness and what God equipped you for is not to be compared to what God designed for man.

Women were created to be producers of life and after the fall, the pain was added to the production. Everything you touch is meant to bring forth life. 1 Corinthians 10:13 NLT states, *"The temptations in your life are no different from what others experience. And God is faithful. He will not allow the temptation to be more than you can stand. When you are tempted, he will show you a way out so that you can endure."* This is a reminder that you will experience some level of pain but God promised that pain would never exceed what He equipped you to bear. This is why the enemy attacks the woman so much because she is a seed (life) bearer. The seed you carry has the capability to crush the head of the enemy. There will be some bruising but the one thing the enemy will never experience that you and I will is the Healing Hand of the Master. You can be healed of and delivered from hurt.

Chapter 10

The First Lady's Trait

"Now the name of the man was Nabal, and the name of his wife, Abigail, and she was a woman of good understanding, and of a beautiful countenance..." (1 Sam. 25:3)

One of my favorite heroines of the bible is Abigail. Her story began with a business proposal that turned bad between her husband, Nabal, and King David. Nabal, whose name means "a fool," is described as a shrewd businessman with no compassion. He is harsh and evil in his doings and hard to deal with. Abigail, whose name means "the father is joyful" or "source of joy," is described as one of good understanding and of a beautiful appearance. Despite their obvious personality differences, these two individuals were joined together as husband and wife.

Abigail brought to this marriage and family two vital traits that I firmly believe every Pastor's Wife must discover she possesses: 1) the strength of character and 2) beauty.

Strength of character is that aspect of you that defines your personality. It is your wit—the intelligence and smartness you

37

bring as a woman into the life of your husband as a man. What he lacks, you complete and what you lack, he completes. It is your courage—those moments where you have to be brave and fight no matter how weary or tired you become. It is your innate discernment—no other woman in the church ministry has this trait other than you First Lady. As the wife of a man who just happens to be a pastor, the Holy Spirit endows you with spiritual perception. This means you will find yourself seeing and catching things in the spirit, some good, some bad, and even some dangerous. What you see does not mean you blab it or allow it to become a bitter root in your heart. Rather, it should provoke you to the posture of prayer.

An incubator is a controlled, protective environment providing light and nourishment for development of premature babies. You are the incubator of prayer, housing your husband, your children, and the ministry. You have the power to bring these things that you see into a spiritual incubator of prayer, seeking the Father to bring forth the change needed. As you make this a daily part of your life, you will find your strength and release. Remember, the change you want to see will first begin with you on your knees in prayer.

Strength of beauty is the trait the Father placed upon every woman. You were created beautiful on purpose. Psalm 139:14 gives the descriptive design of God's treasured creation—man and woman. You and I were God's created masterpiece so distinctly different from any other creature that God set us apart as being extraordinarily beautiful on purpose carrying His nature. Your husband was drawn to your beauty, outwardly and inwardly.

I daily fight to live a balanced life in my busyness. One day I looked in the mirror and said, *"Whew! Girl, you care for others and have forgotten to care for you."* I immediately took some time to get myself back in shape. Why is this important? The answer I am certain you already know: If you fail to take care of you, you will be no good to care for others.

King David, described as a protector, one who is fair, receptive, and the Lord's anointed, attempted to enter into a fair business deal with Nabal but rather than receive his generous offer of goodwill, he insulted him greatly, placing Nabal's entire household in jeopardy of death. Abigail was approached by one of her servants who said, *"Now therefore, know and consider <u>what you will do</u>, for harm is determined against our master and against his entire household." (1 Sam 25:17 NLT).* Abigail had a right to be furious because her husband's actions were about to be the death of her family. However, she chose to operate in the strength of character and beauty for the sake of the family.

There are times in which your husband may make a mistake that will have a devastating effect on the family. You must prayerfully ask the Lord for guidance in how to help rebuild your family, and yes your wounded husband, no matter how much you want to slap him across the forehead. You will have a desire to stay entangled in all of your feelings but your greatest defense, especially in situations like these, is your prayer life.

There has been some financial loss in my own family that took us some time to recover from. To stay sane and saved, my retreat was my prayer closet. That closet birthed many victories. I am not saying I did not hurt because I for sure did. However, lingering hurt brought forth no change, at least on my part. I had to make a choice to no longer allow my emotions to get the best of me and keep me in the bondage of hurt.

I know the enemy has been trying to hold you hostage in hurt but there is too much invested in you and it's called God's grace. So, I ask you, *"What will you do?"* God's grace can help mend those broken pieces in your life. You are the lifeline of your family because God wired you that way. It is why the enemy fights you so hard especially emotionally.

When faced with the potential annihilation of her family, Abigail moved beyond her feelings into her strength of character and beauty and did what was necessary to save her family. When she approached King David, her strength of character and beauty turned a potentially destructive situation into a life-saving victory for her family. The strength of character and beauty you carry has that same ability. Through faith in God and His Word, you have God's power and grace to help make that change.

Chapter 11

Confessions of a First Lady

"Confess your faults one to another, and pray one for another, that ye may be healed." James 5:16

Abigail approached her dilemma head-on in a powerful manner that testifies to her strength of character and beauty. Driven by humility she brought before King David seven confessions (vs. 18-29) that led to victory for her family despite the bad decision made by her husband.

1) *Confession of Forgiveness.* Abigail accepts the blame and repents on behalf of her entire household. I find this interesting because Abigail did not do anything wrong. This act of humility demonstrates the influence a God fearing woman can have in her household. Apostle Paul reminds us that by the witness of your life do you bring holiness into your household. (1 Cor. 7:14)

2) *Confession of Facts.* Abigail makes no excuses for her husband's character but emphatically states, *"My husband is*

who he is." However, you must remember she makes this confession before King David, who is a representation of Jesus Christ, our King. Therefore, your disappointments about your husband's actions are better served in God's ear rather than the public ear. I am in no wise applying that you refrain from seeking necessary wise counsel but cautioning you to not allow your emotions to cause you to operate in a spirit of disrespect. If a change needs to occur, you must yield your faith and prayers to God to be God in the change.

3) *Confession of the Unknown.* Abigail confessed that there were some subsequent consequences that resulted from Nabal's decisions that she was never privy to. There are some aspects of marriage and ministry that will be withheld from you. Do not let this trip you out. Some things you do not need to know. Do not take it personally. If you just have to know, then hit your knees and see what the Holy Ghost reveals to you.

4) *Confession of Reverence.* Abigail boldly proclaims to King David that he is God's choice, anointed and appointed. Your husband may not necessarily tell you, but he really does need your constant affirmation in his life, even when he makes a mistake. Know your husband's roles and responsibilities and honor him for it. Remind him that he is God's choice, anointed and more than able to carry out the Kingdom mandate over his life as a man, husband, father, and pastor.

5) *Confession of Generosity.* Abigail would be remiss if she did not come before the King without a gift. Psalm 96:8 says, *"Give unto the Lord the glory due unto His name. Bring an offering and come into his courts."* You never come into God's presence without a gift. Abigail not only brought forth confessions but she sowed a seed on behalf of her family. She received mercy and favor. There is power in your seed.

6) *Confession of Prophetic Change.* Abigail began to speak prophetically over King David's life. Proverbs 18:21 says, *"Death and life are in the power of the tongue and they that love it shall eat the fruit thereof."* Remember you are the incubator for your family through prayer. Begin to speak life to your husband's destiny in every area of his life.

7) *Confession of Remembrance.* 1 Sam 25:31(b) *"But when the LORD shall have dealt well with my lord, then remember thine handmaid."* As God blessed King David, Abigail asked that he remember her confessions. Abigail teaches us that a woman who walks in the strength of character and beauty has tremendous influence. You will find that as you endeavor to promote your husband, God will remember you. The motivating factor for all seven confessions had to be love. God will honor your confessions and remember your labor of love.

Chapter 12

Be Healed First Lady

"Christ has set us free to live a free life. So take your stand! Never again let anyone put a harness of slavery on you." (Galatians 5:1 Msg)

By cleaving to the hurts in your life, you miss out on great opportunities to cover and protect your husband and your loved ones. The power of prayer and faith in God's Word cannot be measured. They are true weapons of destruction to the tactics of the enemy in your life. You deserve to walk in the freedom of your liberty and the chains of unresolved hurts broken off your life. I encourage you to make a bold-faced decision to implement these practical steps in your life to help you to be the one that understands that although hurts come you can walk in peace for you have learned how to not allow them to take root in your life. Be healed First Lady.

1. Pick up your bible and pray to God to reveal unto you the root issue, not the unresolved issue, but the root issue. Psalm 139:23-24 NLT *"23 Search me, O God, and know my heart; test me and know my anxious thoughts. 24 Point out anything in me that offends you, and lead me along the path of everlasting life."*

2. Pray for wisdom in how to handle the issue. James 1:5 NLT *"If you need wisdom, ask our generous God, and he will give it to you. He will not rebuke you for asking."*

3. Have the mindset of reconciliation. 2 Corinthians 5:18 KJV *"And all things are of God, who hath reconciled us to himself by Jesus Christ, and hath given to us the ministry of reconciliation."*

4. Be merciful without judgment and punishment. Luke 10:37 KJV *"And he said, He that shewed mercy on him. Then said Jesus unto him, Go, and do thou likewise."*

5. Forgive, release and let go. Colossians 3:13 NLT *"Make allowance for each other's faults, and forgive anyone who offends you. Remember, the Lord forgave you, so you must forgive others."*

6. Develop better communication skills DAILY. Ephesians 4:29 NLT *"Don't use foul or abusive language. Let everything you say be good and helpful, so that your words will be an encouragement to those who hear them."*

7. Develop better people skills DAILY. Ephesians 4:2-3 KJV *"² Always be humble and gentle. Be patient with each other, making allowance for each other's faults because of your love. ³ Make every effort to keep yourselves united in the Spirit, binding yourselves together with peace."*

8. Surround yourself with a circle of influence and accountability. Proverbs 11:14 KJV *"Where no counsel is, the people fall: But in the multitude of counsellers there is safety.*

Chapter 13

From the Heart of a First Lady

"And they overcame him by the blood of the Lamb, and by the word of their testimony, and they loved not their lives unto the death."
(Rev. 12:11 KJV)

What greater way to confirm for you First Lady that you are not alone than to let you hear from other Pastors' Wives across the country. From the heart of a First Lady, hear what the voice of experience has to say to encourage you:

♥ "Develop a personal relationship with the Lord. Ask God to give you a Kingdom prayer partner. Keep unity between you and your husband (no matter what happens)." -- *First Lady Phyliss A. Cage, 25 years as a First Lady, God's Tabernacle of Deliverance COGIC, Hammond, Louisiana.* ♥

♥ "Remain in prayer all the time. Never let anyone see you and your husband at odds all the time. Never cause any ruckus before service." -- *Prophetess Wanessa B. Monk, 13 years as a First Lady, Strong Hands Ministries, Lancaster, Texas.* ♥

♥ "Be strong and courageous (Deut. 31:6) because things are not always going to go as planned. Connect with a God-fearing First Lady who will mentor, pray and support you as God instructs from Titus 2:3-5. Stand firm and believe what Romans 8:28 says as you focus and understand your purpose as a wife, a friend, a supporter and a member of the ministry." - *- Co-Pastor Rhoda Wallace, 14 years as a First Lady, City of Worship, Long Beach, California.* ♥

♥ "Make sure God is leading your life and you are obeying God. Love, honor and respect your husband; know that God made Him the head of the church so work with him. Be the First Lady that God called you to be. Love and care for the congregation. Make sure you fellowship with other First Ladies." *-- Prophetess Suella M. Dugar, 25 years as a First Lady, Greater Love Family Worship Center, Crowley, Louisiana.* ♥

♥ "Always be prayerful, especially for your husband. Always be ready to give godly and holy advice to those that are seeking help. Be discreet and graceful. You never know who is looking up to you as a holy role model." *-- First Lady Sally Gilmore, 19 years as a First Lady, Abundant Life Pentecostal Assembly, Boise, Idaho.* ♥

♥ "Everything takes time as God appointed and designated you for this assignment. Much love has to be shown on this journey as you deal with God's people. Your flesh must die to how you feel or think things should be. Love covers." -- *Prophetess Cynthia Brown, 7 years as a First Lady, Harvesting Souls for Christ Ministry, Grand Prairie, Texas.* ♥

♥ "Praise, Pray and Play. You should always keep praise in your heart. Above all else, keep your husband lifted up in prayer and interceding on his behalf as he will face obstacles, adversities, and challenges in the ministry. As you are praying for your husband along with encouraging him, it will strengthen you. Making time to play/have fun with your husband is essential. The ministry can be very demanding at times. There needs to be a moment to rejuvenate and to spend quality time together." -- *First Lady Yolanda Wilson Smith, 13 years as a First Lady, Thy Word Missionary Baptist Church, Fort Worth, Texas.* ♥

♥ "Be who God uniquely designed you to be. There is no blueprint for what a First Lady should be. You have been called and assigned. This is not a position, it is an assignment. Therefore, seek God's guidance in every area of your life. Honor, respect and acknowledge the anointing that is on your husband's life. Be his biggest supporter and encourager. Nurture your marriage and know that it is your first ministry." -- *Evangelist Edwina West Dukes, 9 years as a First Lady, Christ Lifters Community of Faith, Fort Worth, Texas.* ♥

♥ "Becoming the First Lady is just that BECOMING!!! There is no one mold for this position at the side of your husband. It is as individual as you are. The best way for you to be successful in your role as the First Lady is to be yourself. It is challenging enough to serve alongside your husband without struggling within yourself of who you are. You cannot expect to have authentic relationships with God's people through your husband, nor can you use his (your husband's) authority to cause people to do your will. Take the time to get to know the members and use the gifts God has given you to cultivate genuine relationships." -- *First Lady Ericka Davis, 13 years as a First Lady, Jesus is the Answer Apostolic Church, Spokane, Washington.* ♥

♥ "Be in constant prayer and intercession for your marriage, husband, and ministry. Never feel that what you do for the ministry does not matter. Never neglect yourself for the sake of the church." -- *Pastor Versella E. Murray, 21 years as a First Lady, Household of Faith Church Ministries, Fort Worth, Texas.* ♥

♥ "Always pray and listen for God's response. Lead by example. Be yourself, know your strength and acknowledge your weaknesses." -- *Shirelle Brown, 16 years as a First Lady, Prosperity Ministries, Grand Prairie, Texas.* ♥

Conclusion

From My Heart to Yours

As a Pastor's Wife, you are uniquely equipped and designed to fulfill an incredible assignment in serving with your husband, who God has anointed to shepherd His people. You have a calling and a purpose as a woman. I pray that these words have been an encouragement for you to reflect on for the great journey that lies ahead of you. There will be some difficult and lean times, but greater days outweigh the rough days. You can be thankful for knowing that God causes you to *"triumph in Christ, and maketh manifest the savour of his knowledge by [you] in every place."* (2 Cor. 2:14 KJV)

You hold a valuable place in the Kingdom and in your marriage with your husband, the Pastor. May God strengthen you to walk worthy of the calling that God has placed over your life. May your husband embrace and appreciate you as his wife, your voice, your ideas, your gifts, your talents and your call. May your marriage be abundantly blessed, preserved, strengthened, cultivated and fortified to endure all seasons. May your children and the generations after them be successful in the pathway God has laid out for them. May love be the driving force in all your relationships. May the people of the Lord rise, embrace and appreciate the style of your heart as a First Lady.

From my heart to yours,

First Lady Yolanda G. Butler

First Lady Butler Ministries

"Speaking Life One Heart At A Time"

* Evangelist * Intercessor
* Administrator *Author
* Speak Life Determined Coach and Mentor

For speaking engagements or more information please contact
the ministry office:
Co-Pastor Yolanda G. Butler
First Lady Butler Ministries
P. O. Box 60087
Fort Worth, Texas 76115-8087
817-361-8860 Office

email: firstladybutler84@yahoo.com

www.firstladybutlerministries.com
www.praisecentercommunitychurch.org

Made in the USA
Middletown, DE
14 September 2022

10424769R00035